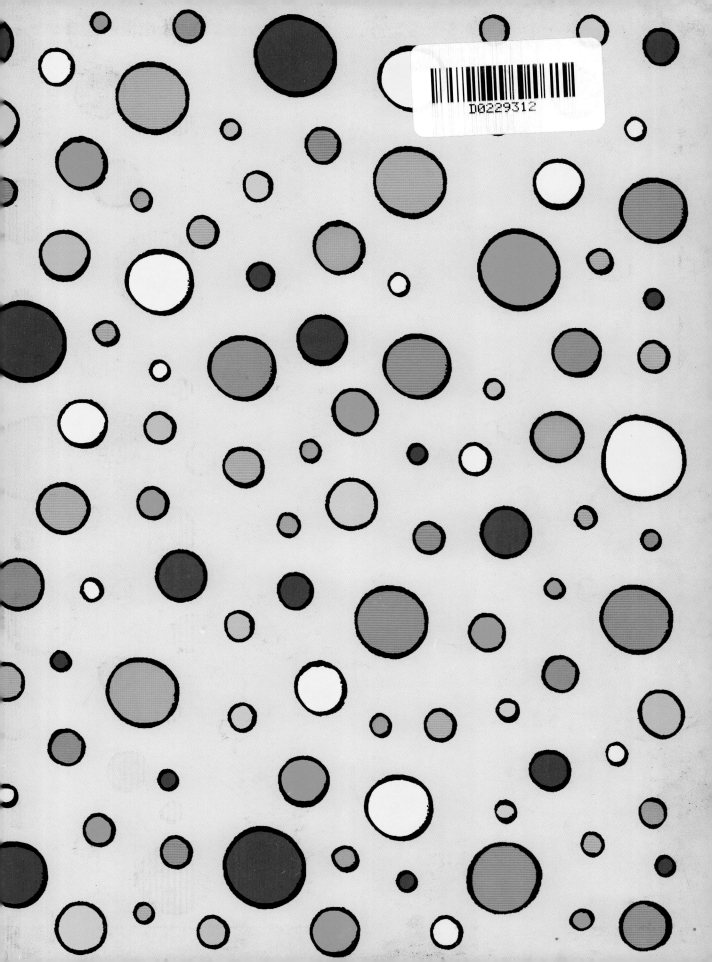

The Puffin Book of Fantastic First Poems

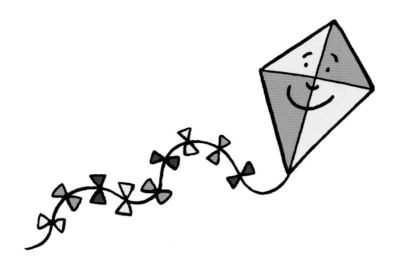

VIKING/PUFFIN

Published by the Penguin Group
Penguin Books Ltd, 27 Wrights Lane, London W8 5TZ, England
Penguin Putnam Inc., 375 Hudson Street, New York, New York 10014, USA
Penguin Books Australia Ltd, Ringwood, Victoria, Australia
Penguin Books Canada Ltd, 10 Alcorn Avenue, Toronto, Ontario, Canada M4V 3B2
Penguin Books (NZ) Ltd, Private Bag 102902, NSMC, Auckland, New Zealand

On the World Wide Web at: www.penguin.com

Penguin Books Ltd, Registered Offices: Harmondsworth, Middlesex, England

First published 1999
1 3 5 7 9 10 8 6 4 2

Printed in Italy by L.E.G.O

British Library Cataloguing in Publication Data
A CIP catalogue record for this book is available from the British Library

ISBN 0–670–88659–9

The Puffin Book of Fantastic First Poems

Edited by June Crebbin

Puffin Books

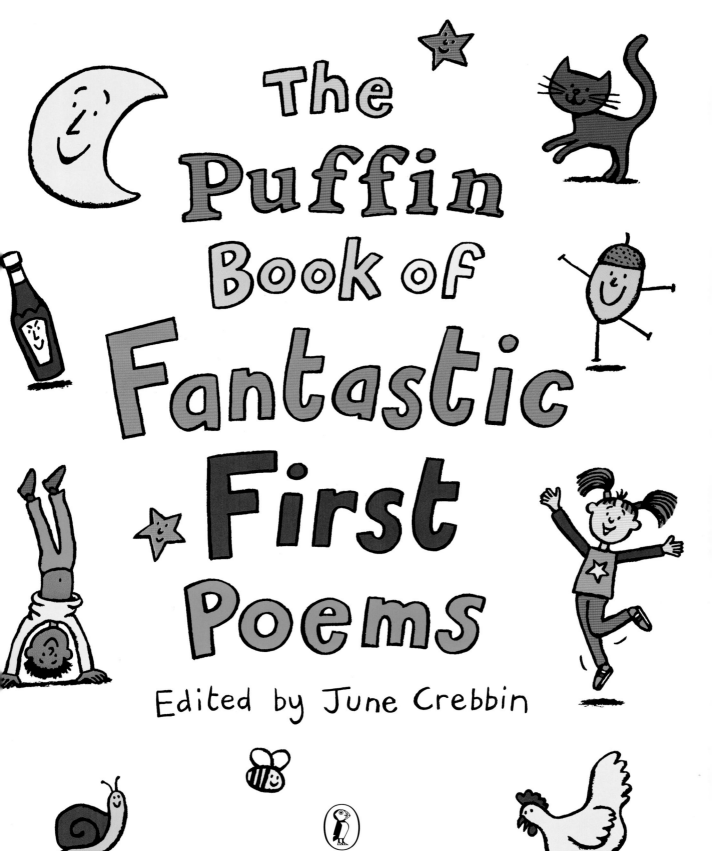

Introduction

One of my earliest memories is standing beside my father's roll-top desk, reciting poems. In front of him was a type-written copy of each poem. As I finished, he typed my name and the date beneath – IN RED! I can still feel the excitement, the honour of the occasion. But more than that, I knew those poems were mine. Many, as with 'From a Railway Carriage', I still know by heart.

Now, I am not suggesting that every child should learn poems by heart, though many will want to, as I did. But those poems were my first poems, my introduction to poetry. Choosing this collection of first poems has given me that same sense of excitement. Here are poems that make me laugh out loud, or conjure up unforgettable images; poems that surprise me, or make me want to tap along with their rhythms; poems that stop me in my tracks, then linger in my mind. I keep grabbing one of my very patient family, or the postman or the rabbit and saying: 'Hey, listen to this – it's fantastic!'

Here you will find ANIMAL poems where you can jigaloo with a kangaroo! PLAYTIME poems where you can breathe dragon smoke or plant your feet on the sky; FAMILY poems, from brothers who are bothers, to dads who almost rescue cats and fall in ponds! FOOD poems where you can slurp your spaghetti or find a golden apple; FUN poems where you can higglety, pigglety, pop or meet a bear – if you dare! OUTINGS poems where you can go looking for a hot spot or take the train to Ricketywick; and BEDTIME poems where you can fold up your thoughts and listen to the moon breathing.

Fantastic first poems for you to sing, shout, whisper, chant – maybe learn by heart! Have fun!

June Crebbin

CONTENTS

HopalooKangaroo
Illustrated by Emily Bolam

Ten Tom-Toms
Illustrated by John Wallace

DADDY FELL INTO THE POND
Illustrated By Emma Chichester Clark

SLURPY SPAGHETTI
Illustrated by Tony Ross

THE TRAIN TO RICKETYWICK
Illustrated by Ann Kronheimer

HIGGLETY, PIGGLETY, POP
Illustrated by Nick Sharratt

I CAN HEAR THE MOON BREATHING
Illustrated by Strawberrie Donnelly

HOPALOO-KANGAROO

Animal Poems

HEN'S SONG

Chick, chick, come out of your shell.
I've warmed you long, and I've warmed you well;
The sun is hot and the sky is blue
Quick, chick, it's time you came through.

Rose Fyleman

ROGER WAS A RAZOR FISH

Roger was a razor fish
as sharp as he could be.
He said to Calvin Catfish,

'I'll shave you for a fee.'

'No thanks,'
said Calvin Catfish,
'I like me like I be.'
And with his whiskers
on his face
he headed out to sea.

Al Pittman

THE TICKLE RHYME

'Who's that tickling my back?' said the wall.
'Me,' said a small
Caterpillar. 'I'm learning
To crawl.'

Ian Serraillier

KITTY

Look at pretty little Kitty
Gnawing on a bone!
How I wish she'd eat some fish
And leave my leg alone.

Doug MacLeod

CAT'S NOTE

How often can you take a poem
   and stroke it on your lap?

John Agard

A DRAGONFLY

When the heat of the summer
Made drowsy the land,
A dragonfly came
And sat on my hand.

With its blue jointed body
And wings like spun glass,
It lit on my fingers
As though they were grass.

Eleanor Farjeon

READY, STEADY – MOO!

It's peaceful here by the river,
All by ourselves in the sun,
Having a chew and a chat now and then,
Moving gently along.

But I'm not too keen on the hikers
That pass through our field each day,
One of them always waves a stick
In a menacing kind of way.

I'm not too keen on their children
Dashing all over the place,
Or their dogs, which run and nip at my heels
And yap in front of my face.

If only they'd just keep going,
If only they'd leave us alone,
Don't they know they're walking through
the middle of our home?

It's time we taught them a lesson,
Yes, but what can we do?
We could try giving voice to the way that we feel:

Ready, steady – MOO-OO-OO!

It's peaceful here by the river
Now that the hikers have gone,
All by ourselves in the meadow again,
Flicking our tails in the sun.

June Crebbin

CATS

Cats sleep
Anywhere,
Any table,
Any chair,
Top of piano,
Window-ledge,
In the middle,
On the edge,
Open drawer,
Empty shoe,
Anybody's
Lap will do,
Fitted in a
Cardboard box,
In the cupboard
With your frocks –
Anywhere!
They don't care!
Cats sleep
Anywhere.

Eleanor Farjeon

DON'T CRY, CATERPILLAR

Don't cry, Caterpillar
Caterpillar, don't cry
You'll be a butterfly – by and by.

Caterpillar, please
Don't worry 'bout a thing

'But,' said Caterpillar,
'Will I still know myself – in wings?'

Grace Nichols

THE TADPOLE

Underneath the water-weeds,
    Small and black, I wriggle,
And life is most surprising!
    Wiggle! waggle! wiggle!
There's every now and then a most
    Exciting change in me,
I wonder, wiggle! waggle!
    What I shall turn out to be.

Elizabeth Gould

HopalooKangaroo

If you can jigaloo
jigaloo
I can do
the jigaloo too
for I'm the jiggiest
jigaloo kangaroo

jigaloo all night through
jigaloo all night through

If you can boogaloo
boogaloo
I can do
the boogaloo too
for I'm the boogiest
boogaloo kangaroo

boogaloo all night through
boogaloo all night through

But bet you can't hopaloo
hopaloo
like I can do
for I'm the hoppiest
hopaloo kangaroo

hopaloo all night through
hopaloo all night through

Gonna show you steps
you never knew.
And guess what, guys?
My baby in my pouch
will be dancing too.

John Agard

Snail

Snail upon the wall,
Have you got at all
Anything to tell
About your shell?

Only this, my child –
When the wind is wild,
Or when the sun is hot,
It's all I've got.

John Drinkwater

TIGER

I'm a tiger
Striped with fur
Don't come near
Or I might Grrr
Don't come near
Or I might growl
Don't come near
Or I might
BITE!

Mary Ann Hoberman

HEY DIDDLE DIDDLE

Hey diddle, diddle,
The cat and the fiddle,
The cow jumped over the moon;
The little dog laughed
To see such fun,
And the dish ran away
with the chocolate biscuits.

Traditional, adapted by Michael Rosen

LITTLE BIRD

Little hurt bird
in my hand
your heart beats
like the pound of the sea
under the warmth
of your soft feathers.

Charlotte Zolotow

FIVE LITTLE OWLS

Five little owls in an old elm tree,
Fluffy and puffy as owls could be,
Blinking and winking with big round eyes
At the big round moon that hung in the skies:
As I passed beneath I could hear one say,
'There'll be mouse for supper, there will, today!'
Then all of them hooted, 'Tu-whit, tu-whoo
Yes, mouse for supper, hoo hoo, hoo hoo!'

Anon

MY DONKEY

His face is what I like.
And his head, much too big for his body – a toy head,
A great, rabbit-eared, pantomime head,
And his friendly rabbit face,
His big, friendly, humorous eyes – which can turn wicked,
Long and devilish, when he lays his ears back.

But mostly he's comical – and that's what I like.
I like the joke he seems.
Always just about to tell me. And the laugh,
The rusty, pump-house engine that cranks up laughter
From some long-ago, far-off, laughter-less desert –

The dry, hideous guffaw
That makes his great teeth nearly fall out.

Ted Hughes

WHISKY FRISKY

Whisky frisky,
Hipperty hop,
Up he goes
To the tree top!

Whirly, twirly,
Round and round,
Down he scampers
To the ground.

Furly, curly,
What a tail,
Tall as a feather,
Broad as a sail.

Where's his supper?
In the shell.
Snappy, cracky,
Out it fell.

Anon

HONEY BEAR

There was a big bear
Who lived in a cave;
His greatest love
Was honey.
He had twopence a week
Which he never could save,
So he never had
Any money.
I bought him a money box
Red and round,
In which to put
His money.
He saved and saved
Till he got a pound,
Then he spent it all
On honey.

Elizabeth Lang

No Hickory No Dickory No Dock

Wasn't me
Wasn't me
said the little mouse
I didn't run up no clock

You could hickory me
You could dickory me
or lock me in a dock

I still say
I didn't run up no clock

Was me who ran under your bed
Was me who bit into your bread
Was me who nibbled your cheese

But please please,
I didn't run up no clock
no hickory
no dickory
no dock.

John Agard

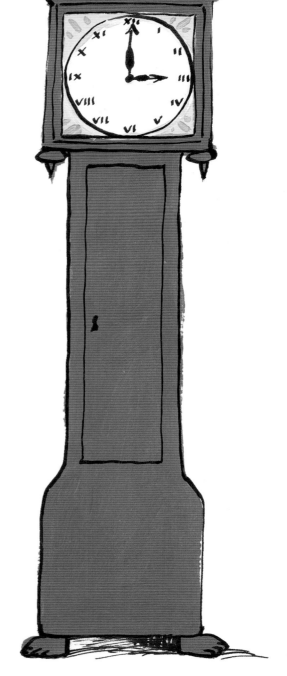

GRANNY GOAT

Eat anything
will granny goat,
handkerchiefs,
the sleeve of your coat,
sandwiches,
a ten pound note,
eat anything
will granny goat.

Granny goat
goes anywhere,
into the house
if you're not there,
follows you round,
doesn't care,
granny goat
goes anywhere.

Granny goat
will not stay
tied up
throughout the day,
chews the rope,
wants to play,
granny goat
won't stay

anywhere you
want her to,
she would rather be
with YOU!

Brian Moses

TEN TOM-TOMS

Poems about Games and Playing

THE WIZARD SAID:

'You find a sheltered spot that faces south . . . '
    'And then?'
'You sniff and put two fingers in your mouth . . . '
    'And then?'
'You close your eyes and roll your eye-balls round . . . '
    'And then?'
'You lift your left foot slowly off the ground . . . '
    'And then?'
'You make your palm into a kind of cup . . . '
    'And then?'
'You *very quickly* raise your right foot up . . . '
    'And then?'
'You fall over.'

Richard Edwards

RUN A LITTLE

Run a little this way,
    Run a little that!
Fine new feathers
    For a fine new hat.
A fine new hat
    For a lady fair –
Run around and turn about
    And jump in the air.

Run a little this way,
    Run a little that!
White silk ribbon
    For a black silk cat.
A black silk cat
    For the Lord Mayor's wife –
Run around and turn about
    And fly for your life!

James Reeves

SOMETIMES

Sometimes
when I skip or hop
or when I'm
    jumping

Suddenly
I like to stop
and listen to me
    thumping.

Lilian Moore

DRAGON SMOKE

Breathe and blow
white clouds
  with every puff.
It's cold today,
  cold enough
to see your breath.
Huff!
  Breathe dragon smoke
    today!

Lilian Moore

Mud

I like mud.
    I like it on my clothes.
I like it on my fingers.
    I like it in my toes.

Dirt's pretty ordinary
    And dust's a dud.
For a really good mess-up
    I like mud.

John Smith

One, Two, Three, Four

One, two, three, four,
Mary at the cottage door,
Eating cherries off a plate,
Five, six, seven, eight.

Anon

CELEBRATION

I shall dance tonight.
When the dusk comes crawling,
There will be dancing
  and feasting.
I shall dance with the others
  in circles,
    in leaps,
      in stomps.
Laughter and talk
  will weave into the night,
Among the fires
  of my people.
Games will be played
And I shall be
  a part of it.

Alonzo Lopez

WE'RE RACING, RACING DOWN THE WALK

We're racing, racing down the walk,
Over the pavements and round the block.
We rumble along till the sidewalk ends –
Felicia and I and half our friends.
Our hair flies backwards. It's whish and whirr!
She roars at me and I shout at her
As past the porches and garden gates
We rattle and rock
On our roller skates.

Phyllis McGinley

HIDEOUT

They looked for me
and from my nook
inside the oak
I watched them look.

Through little slits
between the leaves
I saw their looking
legs and sleeves.

They would have looked
all over town
except –
I threw some acorns down.

Aileen Fisher

FIRST AND LAST

I like to be first in the playground,
I like to stand by the tree,
I like to imagine that all this space
Belongs entirely to me.

I walk from the tree to the waste-bin,
I walk across to the hedge,
I zig-zag across to the bushes
And then I go right round the edge.

When my friends arrive in the playground,
That's when the real games begin.
But I'm not a very fast runner
So I don't often try to join in.

Sometimes they say, 'Are you playing?'
As I practise bouncing my ball,
But they always ask too many people.
I'd rather stay by the wall.

And when I hear the whistle
At precisely five to nine,
And everyone rushes and pushes,
I choose to be last in the line.

I like to be last in the playground,
I take a last look around, and then,
I promise myself that tomorrow
I'll be first in the playground again.

June Crebbin

THE SWING

The wind blows strong and the swing rides free,
And up in the swing is me, is me,
    And the world goes rushing by,
And one of these days I'll swing so far
I'll go way up where the sea birds are
    And plant my feet on the sky.

Marchette Chute

DENS

Dens are where the bears
Sleep the winter away
Or beasts that hunt by night
Lie hidden in the day
Or a den can be
A quilt or eiderdown
Spread from the settee
Over the back of a chair,
A dark and secret place
Where I have made my lair
And you can come to call on me –
If you dare.

Stanley Cook

KITE

A kite on the ground
is just paper and string
but up in the air
it will dance and sing.
A kite in the air
will dance and will caper
but back on the ground
is just string and paper.

Anon

PLACES

There are Go-through places
(Arches and doorways).
There are Crawl-under places
(Fence or wall).
But the Climb-up places
(Clear to the tiptops)
Are the very best places of all!

John Travers Moore

TEN TOM-TOMS

Ten tom-toms,
Timpani, too,
Ten tall tubas
And an old kazoo.

Ten trombones –
Give them a hand!
The sitting-standing-marching-running
Big Brass Band

Anon

ACORN BILL

I made a little acorn man
And inked his smiling face,
I stuck four pins for legs and arms,
Each firmly in its place.

I found a tiny acorn cup
To put upon his head,
And then I showed him to my friends;
'Meet Acorn Bill,' I said.

Ruth Ainsworth

SALT, MUSTARD, VINEGAR, PEPPER

Salt, mustard, vinegar, pepper,
French almond rock,
Bread and butter for your supper
That's all mother's got.
Fish and chips and Coca-Cola,
Put them in a pan,
Irish stew and ice-cream soda,
We'll eat all we can.

Salt, mustard, vinegar, pepper,
French almond rock,
Bread and butter for your supper
That's all mother's got.
Eggs and bacon, salted herring,
Put them in a pot,
Pickled onions, apple pudding,
We will eat the lot.

Salt, mustard, vinegar, pepper,
Pig's head and trout,
Bread and butter for your supper
OUT spells out.

Traditional English

WHAT ARE YOU?

I am a gold lock;
    I am a gold key.
I am a silver lock;
    I am a silver key.
I am a brass lock;
    I am a brass key.
I am a lead lock;
    I am a lead key.
I am a monk lock;
    I am a mon –key.

Traditional

ICE

When it is the winter time
I run up the street
And I make the ice laugh
With my little feet –
'Crickle, crackle, crickle
Crreet, crrreeet, crrreeet.'

Dorothy Aldis

ALL WET

Tommy had a water gun.
He squirted it at Jimmy,
at Jamey, George and Jennifer,
and Katie, Kim and Timmy.
He squirted Sally on the nose.
He squirted Molly on the toes.
He laughed and thought it
lots of fun
till —
Sammy got him
with the hose.

Tony Johnston

MARBLES IN MY POCKET

Marbles in my pocket!
Winter-time's begun!
Marbles in my pocket
That rattle when I run!

Heavy in my pocket
On the way to school;
Smooth against my fingers,
Round and hard and cool;

Marbles in my pocket,
Blue and green and red,
And some are yellow-golden,
And some are brown instead.

Marbles in the playground,
Big and little ring –
Oh, I like playing marbles,
But that's a different thing.

Marbles in my pocket,
Smooth within my hand,
That's the part that's nicest;
Do you understand?

Marbles in my pocket
To rattle when I run!
For winter days are here again,
And marble-time's begun!

Lydia Pender

DADDY FELL INTO THE POND

Family Poems

GIANT

I come up to
My brother's knee.
But that's because
I'm only three.

But when I'm four
I will be able
To see what's on
The kitchen table.

And when I'm five
I know that I
Will be so big
I'll reach the sky.

Clive Webster

GRANDPA

Grandpa's hands are as rough as
    garden sacks
And as warm as pockets.
His skin is crushed paper round
    his eyes
Wrapping up their secrets.

Berlie Doherty

DOUBLE TROUBLE

Sometimes I'm called Katie,
Sometimes I'm called Anne,
This is because most people
Don't know who I am.

It's nice to have a sister,
But the cause of all the trouble
Is I am just like Katie
And Katie is my double.

My uncle says, 'I bet it's fun
Pretending you're each other!'
My aunty wishes one of us
Had been the other's brother!

It's not much fun when my friend Jill
Comes round to have her tea –
She sometimes plays with Katie
Thinking that it's me!

My mum knows what to call me,
My grandad's almost sure
And now there's a way of knowing
We haven't had before,

Katie's lost her two front teeth
So all she has to do
Is smile and grin at everyone –
Then they know who's who!

June Crebbin

DADDY FELL INTO THE POND

Everyone grumbled. The sky was grey.
We had nothing to do and nothing to say.
We were nearing the end of a dismal day.
And there seemed to be nothing beyond.
    Then
        Daddy fell into the pond!

And everyone's face grew merry and bright,
And Timothy danced for sheer delight.
'Give me the camera, quick, oh quick!
He's crawling out of the duckweed!' Click!

Then the gardener suddenly slapped his knee
And doubled up, shaking silently,
And the ducks all quacked as if they were daft,
And it sounded as if the old drake laughed.

Oh, there wasn't a thing that didn't respond
    When
    Daddy fell into the pond!

Alfred Noyes

GRANNY GRANNY PLEASE COMB MY HAIR

Granny Granny
please comb my hair
you always take your time
you always take such care.

You put me to sit on a cushion
between your knees
you rub a little coconut oil
parting gentle as a breeze

Mummy Mummy
she's always in a hurry-hurry
rush
she pulls my hair
sometimes she tugs

But Granny
you have all the time in the world
and when you're finished
you always turn my head and say
'Now who's a nice girl?'

Grace Nichols

GOING THROUGH THE OLD PHOTOS

Who's that?
That's your Auntie Mabel
and that's me
under the table.

Who's that?
That's Uncle Billy.
Who's that?
Me being silly.

Who's that
Licking a lolly?
I'm not sure
but I think it's Polly.

Who's that
behind the tree?
I don't know,
I can't see.
Could be you.
Could be me.

Who's that?
Baby Joe.
Who's that?
I don't know.

Who's that standing
On his head?
Turn it round.
It's Uncle Ted.

Michael Rosen

BILLY IS BLOWING HIS TRUMPET

Billy is blowing his trumpet;
Bertie is banging a tin;
Betty is crying for Mummy
And Bob has pricked Ben with a pin.
Baby is crying out loudly;
He's out on the lawn in his pram.
I am the only one silent
And I've eaten all of the jam.

Anon

THANK YOU, DAD, FOR EVERYTHING

Thank you for laying the carpet, Dad,
Thank you for showing us how,
But what is that lump in the middle, Dad?
And why is it saying mia-ow?

Doug MacLeod

BROTHER

I had a little brother
And I brought him to my mother
And I said I want another
Little brother for a change.
But she said don't be a bother
So I took him to my father
And I said this little bother
Of a brother's very strange.

But he said one little brother
Is exactly like another
And every little brother
Misbehaves a bit he said.
So I took the little bother
From my mother and father
And I put the little bother
Of a brother back to bed.

Mary Ann Hoberman

OUR MOTHER

Our mother is a detective.
She is a great finder of clues.
She found the mud and grass on our shoes,
When we were told not to go in the park –
Because it would be getting dark
But come straight home.

She found the jam on our thumbs,
And in our beds the tiniest crumbs
From the cakes we said we had not eaten.
When we blamed the cat for breaking the fruit bowl –
Because we did not want any fuss –
She *knew* it was us.

Allan Ahlberg

MY SISTER

My sister's remarkably light,
She can float to a fabulous height.
It's a troublesome thing,
But we tie her with string,
And we use her instead of a kite.

Margaret Mahy

NIGHT STARVATION OR THE BITER BIT

At night, my Uncle Rufus
(Or so I've heard it said)
would put his teeth into a glass
Of water by his bed.

At three o'clock one morning
He woke up with a cough,
And as he reached out for his teeth –
They bit his hand right off.

Carey Blyton

MY BROTHER

He giggles and squeaks,
And curls and rolls,
And wriggles and cries,
And screws up his eyes,
And squirms and squeals,
And shouts and yells,
And screeches and begs,
And kicks his legs,
Till Mum puts her head
Round the door and says
'Stop tickling your brother!'

Theresa Heine

DAD AND THE CAT AND THE TREE

This morning a cat got
Stuck in our tree.
Dad said, 'Right, just
Leave it to me.'

The tree was wobbly,
The tree was tall.
Mum said, 'For goodness'
Sake don't fall!'

'Fall?' scoffed Dad,
'A climber like me?
Child's play, this is!
You wait and see.'

He got out the ladder
From the garden shed.
It slipped. He landed
In the flower bed.

'Never mind,' said Dad,
Brushing the dirt
Off his hair and his face
And his trousers and his shirt,

'We'll try Plan B. Stand
Out of the way!'
Mum said, 'Don't fall
Again, OK?'

'Fall again?' said Dad.
'Funny joke!'
Then he swung himself up
On a branch. It broke.

Dad landed *wallop*
Back on the deck.
Mum said, 'Stop it,
You'll break your neck!'

'Rubbish!' said Dad.
'Now we'll try Plan C.
Easy as winking
To a climber like me!'

Then he climbed up high
On the garden wall.
Guess what?
He *didn't fall*!

He gave a great leap
And he landed flat
In the crook of the tree-trunk –
Right on the cat!

The cat gave a yell
And sprang to the ground,
Pleased as punch to be
Safe and sound.

So it's smiling and smirking,
Smug as can be,
But poor old Dad's
Still

Stuck
Up
The
Tree!

Kit Wright

ASK MUMMY ASK DADDY

When I ask Daddy
Daddy says ask Mummy

When I ask Mummy
Mummy says ask Daddy.
I don't know where to go.

Better ask my teddy
he never says no.

John Agard

OH, BABY!

Ever since the baby came
Life at home is not the same,
Of course at first he slept a lot,
Of course my friends and I were not
Supposed to *breathe* in case he woke,
And playing silently's no joke.
We soon found out why all the fuss –
The baby made more noise than us!

Then at mealtimes from his chair
He threw his dinner everywhere –
Peas and ham went whizzing by,
Soggy custard, apple pie –
My dad and I soon learnt to duck,
My mother said: 'With any luck,
He'll soon be past this stage and then
We'll all enjoy our food again.'

He's talking now and drives me dotty
Shuffling round me on his potty,
Wanting me to stay and play,
Repeating everything I say –
Still, though I'm not too certain
Just what it is about him,
Despite his crazy antics,
I wouldn't be without him.

June Crebbin

DAD

Dad is the dancing-man
The laughing-bear, the prickle-chin,
The tickle-fingers, jungle-roars
Bucking bronco, rocking-horse,
The helicopter roundabout
The beat-the-wind at swing-and-shout
Goal-post, scarey-ghost
Climbing-Jack, humpty-back.

But sometimes he's
A go-away-please!
A snorey-snarl, a sprawly slump
A yawny mouth, a sleeping lump,

And I'm a kite without a string
Waiting for Dad to dance again.

Berlie Doherty

A MUSICAL FAMILY

I can play the piano
I am nearly three.
I can play the long white note
That Mum calls Middle C.

Dad can play the clarinet.
My sister plays the fiddle,
But I'm the one who hits the piano
Slap bang in the middle.

John Mole

GOODNESS GRACIOUS!

Goodness gracious, fiddle dee dee!
Somebody's grandmother out at sea!

Just where the breakers begin to bound
Somebody's grandmother bobbing around.

Up on the shore the people shout,
'Give us a hand and we'll pull you out!'

'No!' says the granny, 'I'm right as rain,
And I'm going to go on till I get to Spain.'

Margaret Mahy

Slurpy Spaghetti

Food Poems

ON TOMATO KETCHUP

If you do not shake the bottle,
None'll come, and then a lot'll.

Anon

SOUNDS GOOD!

Sausage sizzles,
crispbreads crack;
hot dogs hiss
and flapjacks snap!

Bacon boils
and fritters fry;
apples squelch
in apple pie.

Baked beans bubble,
gravy grumbles;
popcorn pops,
and stomach rumbles . . .

I'M HUNGRY!

Judith Nicholls

BIG BERT

Big Bert sat on a cushion,
'I'm much too fat,' moaned he,
'Who else could be so miserable?'
The cushion answered: 'Me!'

Richard Edwards

PEAS

I eat my peas with honey,
I've done it all my life,
They do taste kind of funny,
But it keeps them on the knife.

Anon

THE DINOSAUR'S DINNER

Once a mighty dinosaur
Came to dine with me,
He gobbled up the curtains
And swallowed our settee.

He didn't seem to fancy
Onion soup with crusty bread,
He much preferred the flavour
Of our furniture instead.

He ate up all our dining-chairs
And carpets from the floor,
He polished off the table, then
He looked around for more.

The television disappeared
In one almighty gulp,
Wardrobes, beds and bathroom
He crunched into a pulp.

He really loved the greenhouse,
He liked the garden shed,
He started on the chimney-pots
But then my mother said:

'Your friends are always welcome
To drop in for a bite,
But really this one seems to have
A giant appetite.

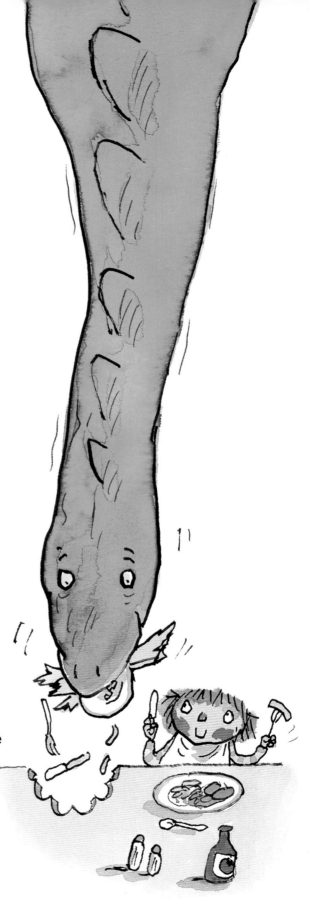

You'd better take him somewhere else,
I'm sure I don't know where,
I only know this friend of yours
Needs more than we can spare!'

And suddenly I realized
I knew the very place,
And when I showed him where it was
You should have seen his face –

I don't think I've seen anyone
Enjoy a dinner more,
I watched him wander on his way,
A happy dinosaur!

The council did rebuild our school,
But that of course took time . . .
And all because a dinosaur
Came home with me to dine!

June Crebbin

THE PANCAKE

Mix a pancake,
Stir a pancake,
    Pop it in the pan.

Fry the pancake,
Toss the pancake,
    Catch it if you can.

Christina Rossetti

DINNER-TIME RHYME

Can you tell me, if you please,
Who it is likes mushy peas?
    Louise likes peas.
How about Sam?
    Sam likes Spam.
How about Vince?
    Vince likes mince.
How about Kelly?
    Kelly likes jelly.
How about Trish?
    Trish likes fish.
How about Pips?
    Pips likes chips.
How about Pete?
    Pete likes meat.
How about Sue?
    Sue likes stew.
How about Greg?
    Greg likes egg.
How about Pam?
    Pam likes lamb.

OK, then, tell me, if you can –
How about Katerina Wilhelmina Theodora Dobson?

    She goes home for dinner . . .

June Crebbin

TOASTER TIME

Tick tick tick tick tick tick tick
Toast up a sandwich quick quick quick
Hamwich
Jamwich
Lick lick lick!

Tick tick tick tick tick tick — stop!
  Pop!

Eve Merriam

PORRIDGE IS BUBBLING

Porridge is bubbling,
Bubbling hot,
Stir it round
And round in the pot.
The bubbles plip!
The bubbles plop!
It's ready to eat
All bubbling hot.

Anon

Breakfast

Good morning little earthworm
said the speckled Thrush
Where would you be going
so early in a rush
I'm off to find some breakfast
he answered with a frown
Well so am I sir said the Thrush
and quickly gulped him down.

P. H. Kilby

I'M AN APPLE

I'm a red apple.
Eat me.
Chew me and chomp me,
Sweetly.
Pick me and peel me,
But buy me, don't steal me,
For I'm a red apple,
Eat me.

I'm a green apple,
Bake me.
Into hot pies and sweet puddings
Make me.
Cut me and core me,
But please don't ignore me,
For I'm a green apple,
Bake me.

I'm a gold apple.
Leave me.
Don't pluck me, and please don't be
Greedy.
You've eaten too much,
So don't snatch and don't touch.
Let me stay in the sunlight,
Leave me.

Clive Riche

SOGGY GREENS

Oh, soggy greens I hate you,
I hate your sloppy slush;
And if my mum would let me,
I'd throw you in a bush.

Oh, apple pie I love you,
I love your crunchy crust;
And if my mum would let me,
I'd eat you till I bust.

John Cunliffe

SPAGHETTI! SPAGHETTI!

Spaghetti! spaghetti!
you're wonderful stuff,
I love you, spaghetti,
I can't get enough.
You're covered with sauce
and you're sprinkled with cheese,
spaghetti! spaghetti!
oh, give me some please.

Spaghetti! spaghetti!
piled high in a mound,
you wiggle, you wriggle,
you squiggle around.
There's slurpy spaghetti
all over my plate,
spaghetti! spaghetti!
I think you are great.

Spaghetti! spaghetti!
I love you a lot,
you're slishy, you're sloshy,
delicious and hot,
I gobble you down
oh, I can't get enough,
spaghetti! spaghetti!
you're wonderful stuff.

Jack Prelutsky

THE WOBBLING RACE

Two jellies had a wobbling race
To see who was the wibbliest.
Then the sun came out and melted them
And made them both the dribbliest.

Clive Riche

HUMPTY DUMPTY

Humpty Dumpty sat on a wall,
Eating black bananas.
Where do you think he put the skins?
Down the king's pyjamas.

Anon

SUGARCAKE BUBBLE

Sugarcake, Sugarcake
   Bubbling in a pot
Bubble, Bubble Sugarcake
   Bubble thick and hot

Sugarcake, Sugarcake
   Spice and coconut
Sweet and sticky
   Brown and gooey

I could eat the lot.

Grace Nichols

THE TRAIN TO RICKETYWICK

Poems about Holidays and Days Out

THE PARK

I'm glad that I
    Live near a park
For in the winter
    After dark
The park lights shine
    As bright and still
As dandelions
    On a hill.

James S. Tippett

THE PASTURE

I'm going out to clean the pasture spring;
I'll only stop to rake the leaves away
(And wait to watch the water clear, I may):
I sha'n't be gone long. – You come too.

I'm going out to fetch the little calf
That's standing by the mother. It's so young
It totters when she licks it with her tongue.
I sha'n't be gone long. – You come too.

Robert Frost

MY GRANNIES

I hate it, in the holiday,
When Grandma brings her pets to stay –
He goat, her pig, her seven rats
Scare our dog and chase our cats.
Her budgies bite, her parrots shout –
And guess who has to clean them out?

My other Gran, the one I like,
Always brings her motor-bike,
And when she takes me for a ride
To picnic in the countryside,
We zoom up hills and whizz round bends –
I hate it when her visit ends!

June Crebbin

BUSY DAY

Pop in
pop out
pop over the road
pop out for a walk
pop in for a talk
pop down to the shop
can't stop
got to pop

got to pop?

pop where?
pop what?

well
I've got to
pop round
pop up
pop in to town
pop out and see
pop in for tea
pop down to the shop
can't stop
got to pop

got to pop?

pop where?
pop what?

well
I've got to
pop in
pop out
pop over the road
pop out for a walk
pop in for a talk . . .

Michael Rosen

UNTIL I SAW THE SEA

Until I saw the sea
I did not know
that wind
could wrinkle water so.

I never knew
that sun
could splinter a whole sea of blue.

Nor
did I know before,
a sea breathes in and out
upon a shore.

Lilian Moore

SUMMER DAYS

I'm looking for a hot spot.
A what spot?
A hot spot.
I'm looking for a hot spot.
To lie out in the sun.
I'm looking for a hot spot
To play and have some fun.
I'm looking for a hot spot
To hit a ball and run.
Oh, I'm looking for a hot spot.
A what spot?
A hot spot.
I'm looking for a hot spot
Now summer has begun.

Anne English

RICKETY TRAIN RIDE

I'm taking the train to Ricketywick.
Clickety clickety clack.
I'm sat in my seat
with a sandwich to eat
as I travel the trickety track.

It's an ever so rickety trickety train,
and I honestly thinkety think
that before it arrives
at the end of the line
it will tip up my drippety drink.

Tony Mitton

IF I COULD ONLY TAKE HOME A SNOWFLAKE

Snowflakes
like tiny
insects
drifting
down.

Without a hum
they come,
Without a hum
they go.

Snowflakes
like tiny
insects
drifting
down.

If only
I could take
one
home with me
to show
my friends
in the sun,
just for fun,
just for fun.

John Agard

SUMMER SONG

By the sand between my toes,
By the waves behind my ears,
By the sunburn on my nose,
By the little salty tears
That make rainbows in the sun
When I squeeze my eyes and run,
By the way the seagulls screech,
Guess where I am? *At the* . . . . . . !
By the way the children shout
Guess what happened? *School is* . . . . . !
By the way I sing this song
Guess if summer lasts too long:
You must answer *Right or* . . . . . !

John Ciardi

FROM A RAILWAY CARRIAGE

Faster than fairies, faster than witches,
Bridges and houses, hedges and ditches;
And charging along like troops in a battle,
All through the meadows the horses and cattle:
All of the sights of the hill and the plain
Fly as thick as driving rain;
And ever again, in the wink of an eye,
Painted stations whistle by.

Here is a child who clambers and scrambles,
All by himself and gathering brambles;
Here is a tramp who stands and gazes;
And there is the green for stringing the daisies!
Here is a cart run away in the road,
Lumping along with man and load;
And here is a mill, and there is a river;
Each a glimpse and gone for ever!

Robert Louis Stevenson

BIKING

Fingers grip,
toes curl;
head down,
wheels whirl.

Hair streams,
fields race;
ears sting,
winds chase.

Breathe deep,
troubles gone;
just feel
windsong.

Judith Nicholls

COBWEB MORNING

On a Monday morning
We do spellings and Maths.
And silent reading.

But on the Monday
After the frost
We went straight outside.

Cobwebs hung in the cold air,
Everywhere.
All around the playground,
They clothed the trees,
Dressed every bush
In veils of fine white lace.

Each web,
A wheel of patient spinning.
Each spider,
Hidden,
Waiting.

Inside,
We worked all morning
To capture the outside.

Now
In our patterns and poems
We remember
The cobweb morning.

June Crebbin

THERE ARE BIG WAVES

There are big waves and little waves,
    Green waves and blue,
Waves you can jump over,
    Waves you dive thro',
Waves that rise up
    Like a great water wall,
Waves that swell softly
    And don't break at all,
Waves that can whisper,
    Waves that can roar,
And tiny waves that run at you
    Running on the shore.

Eleanor Farjeon

75

PICNIC

George, lend a hand
and spread that cloth,
the sand is everywhere!
Just look at that,
you'd never think
it took hours to prepare!

WAKE UP, GRAMP!
Your food's all out,
get it while you can!
Have a lemonade before
it warms in the sun.

What is it, Mum?

There's ...

*ham with sand,
and Spam with sand,
there's chicken paste
and lamb with sand;
oranges, bananas,
lemonade or tea;
bread with sand
all spread with sand –
at least the sand comes free!
We've crisps with sand
and cake with sand –*

it's grand with lunch or tea –
crunch it up,
enjoy it, love,
at least we're by the sea!

Judith Nicholls

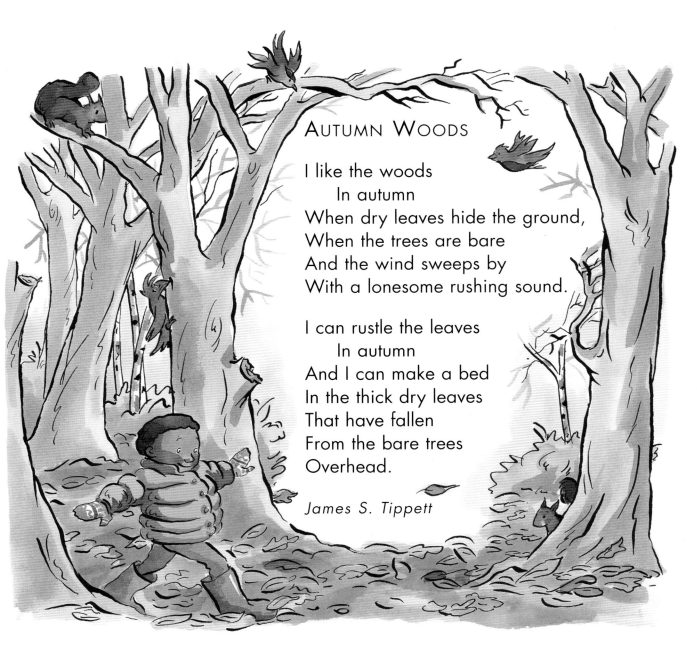

AUTUMN WOODS

I like the woods
    In autumn
When dry leaves hide the ground,
When the trees are bare
And the wind sweeps by
With a lonesome rushing sound.

I can rustle the leaves
    In autumn
And I can make a bed
In the thick dry leaves
That have fallen
From the bare trees
Overhead.

James S. Tippett

LISTEN

Shhhhhhhhh!
Sit still, very still
And listen.
Listen to wings
Lighter than eyelashes
Stroking the air.
Know what the thin breeze
Whispers on high
To the coconut trees.
Listen and hear.

Telcine Turner

HOLIDAY MEMORIES

When I was on holiday
I went to Timbuktu,
I wrestled with a jaguar
And boxed a kangaroo.

I journeyed into jungles,
I swam the deepest sea,
I climbed the highest mountain
And a monkey-puzzle tree.

I chatted to a seagull,
I met a big baboon,
I floated on a moonbeam
Until I reached the moon.

I visited the planets,
I lit up all the stars,
I gossiped to a parrot
Travelling to Mars.

I sailed across the ocean,
I drove a Greyhound bus,
I rode across the desert
On a hippopotamus.

I heard a mermaid singing,
I fought a killer shark,
I grappled with a Grizzly
In a wild Safari Park.

I chased a band of pirates
Completely round the bend.
And now the summer's over
And so is this – THE END.

June Crebbin

GONE

I had it today
For just an hour,
Then, tugged away
By the wind's power
It sailed off free
Above the crowd,
High as a tree,
High as a cloud,
High as the moon,
High as the sun,
My blue balloon
Has gone, gone, gone.

Eric Finney

HIGGLETY, PIGGLETY, POP

Fun and Nonsense Poems

THE OLD MAN OF PERU

There was an old man of Peru,
Who dreamt he was eating his shoe.
    He woke in the night
    In a terrible fright,
And found it was perfectly true.

Anon

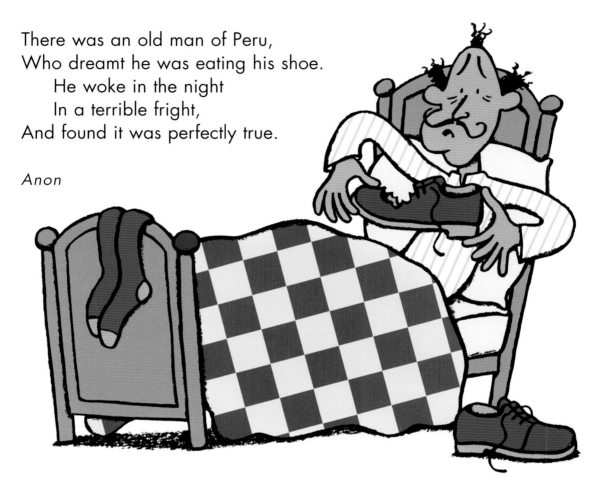

HIGGLETY, PIGGLETY, POP

Higglety, pigglety, pop!
The dog has eaten the mop;
The pig's in a hurry,
The cat's in a flurry,
Higglety, pigglety, pop!

Unknown

My Name Is ...

My name is Sluggery-wuggery
My name is Worms-for-tea
My name is Swallow-the-table-leg
My name is Drink-the-Sea
My name is I-eat-saucepans
My name is I-like-snails
My name is Grand-piano-George
My name is I-ride-whales.
My name is Jump-the-chimney
My name is Bite-my-knee
My name is Jiggery-pokery
And Riddle-me-ree,
and me

Pauline Clarke

No Harm Done

As I went out
The other day,
My head fell off
And rolled away.

But when I noticed
It was gone,
I picked it up
And put it on.

Anon

YAN, TAN, TETHER

Yan, tan, tether, mether, pimp.
Sether, hether, hother, dother, dick.
Yan dick, tan dick, tether dick, mether dick, bumfit.
Yan bumfit, tan bumfit, tether bumfit, mether bumfit, gigot.

Anon
Cumbrian way of counting sheep: one to twenty.

ELETELEPHONY

Once there was an elephant,
Who tried to use the telephant –
No! No! I mean an elephone
Who tried to use the telephone –
(Dear me! I am not certain quite
That even now I've got it right.)

Howe'er it was, he got his trunk
Entangled in the telephunk;
The more he tried to get it free,
The louder buzzed the telephee –
(I fear I'd better drop the song
Of elephop and telephong!)

Anon

NUTTER

The moon's a big white football,
The sun's a pound of butter.
The earth is going round the twist
And I'm a little nutter!

Kit Wright

AS I WAS GOING UP THE STAIR

As I was going up the stair
I met a man who wasn't there.
He wasn't there again today.
Oh, how I wish he'd go away!

Anon

A CHUBBY LITTLE SNOWMAN

A chubby little snowman
Had a carrot nose;
Along came a rabbit
And what do you suppose?
That hungry little bunny,
Looking for his lunch,
ATE the snowman's carrot nose . . .
Nibble, nibble, CRUNCH!

Anon

ALGY

Algy met a bear,
A bear met Algy.
The bear was bulgy,
The bulge was Algy.

Anon

PLEAS-E!

Bumble bee, bumble bee,
Fly away home;
Leave my naked toes
Alone!

Bumble bee, bumble bee,
Don't you know
Another place where
You can go?

Bumble bee, bumble bee,
When I doze off,
I don't need you, so
Buzz off!

June Crebbin

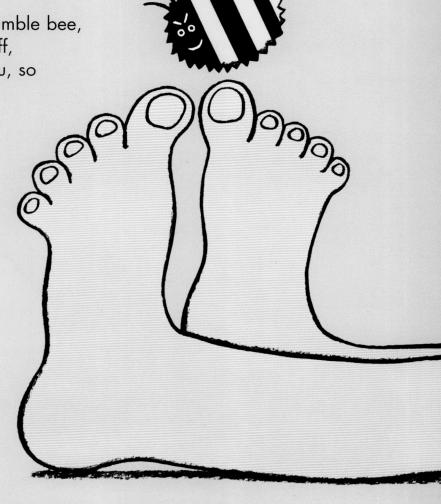

My Dad's Thumb

My dad's thumb
can stick pins in wood
without flinching –
it can crush family-size matchboxes
in one stroke
and lever off jam-jar lids without piercing
at the pierce here sign.

If it wanted
it could be a bath-plug
or a paint-scraper
a keyhole cover or a tap-tightener.

It's already a great nutcracker
and if it dressed up
it could easily pass
as a broad bean or a big toe.

In actual fact, it's quite simply
the world's fastest envelope burster.

Michael Rosen

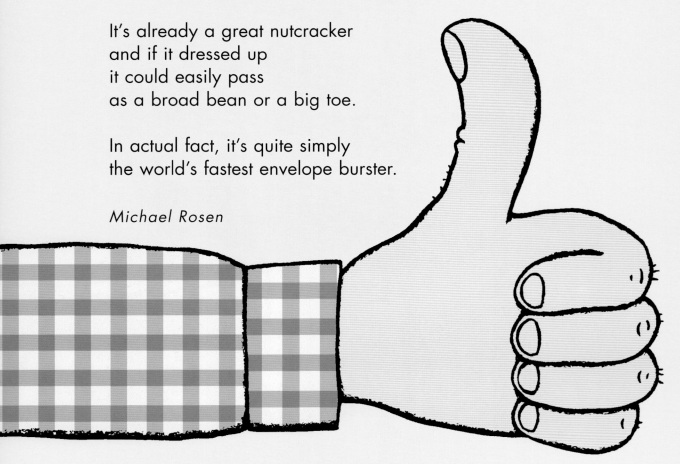

WHO'S IN?

'The door is shut fast
And everybody's out.
But people don't know
What they're talking about!'
Say the fly on the wall,
And the flame on the coals,
And the dog on his rug,
And the mice in their holes,
And the kitten curled up,
And the spiders that spin –
'What, everyone out?
Why, everyone's in!'

Elizabeth Fleming

THE KETTLE

There's a little metal kettle
That is sitting near the settle.
You will hear the tittle tattle
Of the lid begin to rattle
When the kettle starts to boil.
What a pretty prittle prattle
Of the kettle near the settle,
Such a merry tittle tattle
When the lid begins to rattle
And the kettle starts to boil.

Gwynneth Thurburn

AWKWARD CHILD

She fell into the bath-tub
She fell into the sink,
She fell into the raspberry jam
And came – out – pink.

Rose Fyleman

A BOY WENT WALKING

One day a boy went walking,
And walked into a store.
He bought a pound of sausage meat,
And laid it on the floor.

The boy began to whistle –
He whistled up a tune,
And all the little sausages
Danced around the room.

Unknown

WITCH, WITCH

'Witch, witch, where do you fly?'. . .
'Under the clouds and over the sky.'

'Witch, witch, what do you eat?'. . .
'Little black apples from Hurricane Street.'

'Witch, witch, what do you drink?'. . .
'Vinegar, blacking and good red ink.'

'Witch, witch, where do you sleep?'. . .
'Up in the clouds where pillows are cheap.'

Rose Fyleman

FOUR STIFF-STANDERS

Four stiff-standers
Four dilly-danders,
Two lookers,
Two crookers
And a wig-wag.

Traditional

CLOCKS AND WATCHES

Our great
Steeple clock
Goes TICK – TOCK,
TICK – TOCK;

Our small
Mantel clock
Goes TICK–TACK, TICK–TACK,
TICK–TACK, TICK–TACK;

Our little
Pocket watch
Goes Tick-a-tacker, tick-a-tacker
Tick-a-tacker, tick.

Unknown

THERE WAS AN OLD WOMAN

There was an old woman who lived under a hill,
And if she's not gone, she's living there still.

Unknown

I Can Hear the Moon Breathing

Bedtime Poems

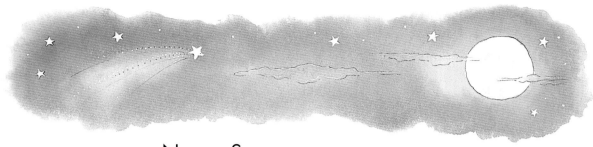

NIGHT SOUNDS

When I lie in bed
I think I can hear
The stars being switched on
I think I can.

And I think I can hear
The moon
Breathing.

But I have to be still.
So still.
All the house is sleeping.
Except for me.

Then I think I can hear it.

Berlie Doherty

MRS MOON

Mrs Moon
sitting up in the sky
Little Old Lady
rock-a-bye
with a ball of fading light
and silvery needles
knitting the night.

Roger McGough

TEDDY BEAR, TEDDY BEAR

Teddy Bear, Teddy Bear,
Go upstairs.
Teddy Bear, Teddy Bear,
Say your prayers.
Teddy Bear, Teddy Bear,
Turn out the light.
Teddy Bear, Teddy Bear,
Say good night.

Anon

FROM THE BED BOOK

Beds come in all sizes –
Single or double,
Cot-size or cradle,
King-size or trundle.

Most Beds are Beds
For sleeping or resting,
But the *best* Beds are much
More interesting!

Not just a white little
Tucked-in-tight little
Nighty-night little
Turn-out-the-light little
  Bed –

  Instead
A Bed for Fishing,
A Bed for Cats,
A Bed for a Troupe of
  Acrobats.

The *right* sort of Bed
(If you see what I mean)
Is a Bed that might
Be a Submarine

Nosing through water
Clear and green,
Silver and glittery
As a sardine

Or a Jet-Propelled Bed
For visiting Mars
With mosquito nets
For the shooting stars . . .

Sylvia Plath

THE HORSEMAN

I heard a horseman
Ride over the hill;
The moon shone clear,
The night was still;
His helm was silver,
And pale was he,
And the horse he rode
Was of ivory.

Walter de la Mare

BEDTIME

Five minutes, five minutes more, please!
  Let me stay five minutes more!
Can't I just finish the castle
  I'm building here on the floor?
Can't I just finish the story
  I'm reading here in my book?
Can't I just finish this bead-chain –
  It *almost* is finished, look!
Can't I just finish the game, please?
  When a game's once begun
It's a pity never to find out
  Whether you've lost or won.
Can't I just stay five minutes?
  Well, can't I stay just four?
Three minutes, then? two minutes?
  Can't I stay *one* minute more?

Eleanor Farjeon

STAR LIGHT, STAR BRIGHT

Star light, star bright,
First star I see tonight,
I wish I may, I wish I might,
Have the wish I wish tonight.

Traditional

SILVER

Slowly, silently, now the moon
Walks the night in her silver shoon;
This way, and that, she peers, and sees
Silver fruit upon silver trees;
One by one the casements catch
Her beams beneath the silvery thatch;
Couched in his kennel, like a log,
With paws of silver sleeps the dog;
From their shadowy cote the white breasts peep
Of doves in silver-feathered sleep;
A harvest mouse goes scampering by,
With silver claws, and silver eye;
And moveless fish in the water gleam,
By silver reeds in a silver stream.

Walter de la Mare

FROM HIAWATHA'S CHILDHOOD

By the shores of Gitche Gumee,
By the shining Big-Sea-Water,
Stood the wigwam of Nokomis,
Daughter of the Moon, Nokomis.
Dark behind it rose the forest,
Rose the black and gloomy pine-trees,
Rose the firs with cones upon them;
Bright before it beat the water,
Beat the clear and sunny water,
Beat the shining Big-Sea-Water.
There the wrinkled, old Nokomis
Nursed the little Hiawatha,
Rocked him in his linden cradle,
Bedded soft in moss and rushes,
Safely bound with reindeer sinews;
Stilled his fretful wail by saying,
'Hush! the Naked Bear will hear thee!'
Lulled him into slumber, singing,
'Ewa-yea! my little owlet!
Who is this, that lights the wigwam?
With his great eyes lights the wigwam?
Ewa-yea! my little owlet!'

Longfellow

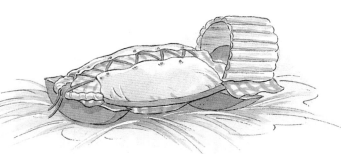

LADYBIRD! LADYBIRD!

Ladybird! Ladybird! Fly away home,
Night is approaching, and sunset is come:
The herons are flown to their trees by the Hall;
Felt, but unseen, the damp dewdrops fall.
This is the close of a still summer day;
Ladybird! Ladybird! haste! fly away.

Emily Brontë

CATAPILLOW

A catapillow
is a useful pet

To keep
upon your bed

Each night you simply
fluff him up

Then rest
your weary head.

Roger McGough

MY TEDDY HAS A FRIGHT

Sometimes my teddy
has a fright
when there's a squeak
or creak at night,
so I cuddle him
and hold him tight,
until he says
he feels all right.

Charles Thomson

FROM NIGHT

The sun descending in the west,
The evening star does shine;
The birds are silent in their nest,
And I must seek for mine.
The moon, like a flower,
In heaven's high bower,
With silent delight
Sits and smiles on the night.

William Blake

BED IN SUMMER

In winter I get up at night
And dress by yellow candle-light.
In summer, quite the other way,
I have to go to bed by day.

I have to go to bed and see
The birds still hopping on the tree,
Or hear the grown-up people's feet
Still going past me in the street.

And does it not seem hard to you,
When all the sky is clear and blue,
And I should like so much to play,
To have to go to bed by day?

Robert Louis Stevenson

At Night

When night is dark
my cat is wise
to light the lanterns
in his eyes.

Aileen Fisher

Going to Sleep

Going to sleep is a funny thing,
I lie in bed and I'm yawning
and Dad is reading a story and then . . .

Suddenly it's morning!

Ian McMillan

GOOD NIGHT, GOOD NIGHT

The dark is dreaming.
    Day is done.
Good night, good night
    To everyone.

Good night to the birds,
    And the fish in the sea,
Good night to the bears
    And good night to me.

Dennis Lee

THE DARK

I don't like the dark coming down on my head
It feels like a blanket thrown over the bed
I don't like the dark coming down on my head

I don't like the dark coming down over me
It feels like the room's full of things I can't see
I don't like the dark coming down over me

There isn't enough light from under the door
It only just reaches the edge of the floor
There isn't enough light from under the door

I wish that my dad hadn't put out the light
It feels like there's something that's just out of sight
I wish that my dad hadn't put out the light

But under the bedclothes it's warm and secure
You can't see the ceiling you can't see the floor
Yes, under the bedclothes it's warm and secure
So I think I'll stay here till it's daylight once more.

Adrian Henri

GOOD NIGHT

Now good night.
Fold up your clothes
As you were taught,
Fold your two hands,
Fold up your thought;
Day is the plough-land,
Night is the stream,
Day is for doing
And night is for dream.
Now good night.

Eleanor Farjeon

INDEX OF FIRST LINES

INDEX OF FIRST LINES

ACKNOWLEDGEMENTS

'Ask Mummy Ask Daddy' and 'If I Could Only Take Home a Snowflake' from *I Din Do Nuttin* by John Agard (The Bodley Head, 1991) c/o Caroline Sheldon Literary Agency; 'Cat's Note' and 'HopalooKangaroo' from *We Animals Would Like a Word With You* by John Agard (The Bodley Head, 1996) c/o Caroline Sheldon Literary Agency; 'No Hickory No Dickory No Dock' from *No Hickory No Dickory No Dock* (Viking, 1991). All by kind permission of John Agard c/o Caroline Sheldon Literary Agency; 'Our Mother' from *Please Mrs Butler* by Allan Ahlberg (Kestrel, 1983), copyright © Allan Ahlberg, 1983, reprinted by permission of Penguin Books Ltd; 'Acorn Bill' by Ruth Ainsworth, reprinted by permission of R. F. Gilbert; 'Ice' from *Everything and Anything* by Dorothy Aldis, copyright 1925–1927, renewed 1953, © 1954, 1955 by Dorothy Aldis, used by permission of G.P. Putnam's Sons, a division of Penguin Putnam Inc.; 'Summer Song' from *The Song of the Sillies* (J. B. Lippincott Co, 1961) by John Ciardi, reprinted by permission of Myra J. Ciardi on behalf of the family of John Ciardi; 'My Name is …' by Pauline Clarke from *Silver Bells and Cockle Shells*, © Pauline Clark 1962, reproduced by permission of Curtis Brown Ltd, London; 'Dens' from *The Poem Box* by Stanley Cook (Blackie, 1991), copyright © the estate of Stanley Cook, 1991, permission granted by Mrs S. Matthews; 'Cobweb Mornings', 'Dinner-time Rhyme', 'First and Last', 'My Grannies' and 'Pleas-e!' from *The Jungle Sale* (Viking, 1988) by June Crebbin, 'Double Trouble', 'Holiday Memories', 'Oh, Baby!' and 'The Dinosaur's Dinner' from *The Dinosaur's Dinner* (Viking, 1992) by June Crebbin, 'Ready, Steady, Moo!' from *Cows Moo, Cars Toot* (Viking, 1995) by June Crebbin, copyright © June Crebbin 1988, 1992 & 1995, reprinted by permission of the author and Penguin Books Ltd; 'Soggy Greens' © 1991 John Cunliffe, first published by Andre Deutsch Publishers, reprinted by permission of David Higham Associates Ltd; 'Dad', 'Grandpa' and 'Night Sounds' from *Walking on Air* (HarperCollins, 1993) by Berlie Doherty, reprinted by permission of David Higham Associates Ltd; 'Snail' by John Drinkwater, copyright © 1929 by John Drinkwater, permission granted by Samuel French, Inc.; 'Big Bert' and 'The Wizard Said' by Richard Edwards from *Whispers in a Wardrobe* (The Lutterworth Press), reprinted by permission of James Clarke & Co. Ltd, The Lutterworth Press; 'Summer Days' by Anne English from *Poetry Corner (Teacher's Notes) Radio* (BBC, 1978), copyright © Anne English 1978, reprinted by permission of Anne B English; 'Cats' by Eleanor Farjeon from *The Children's Bells* (OUP), 'Bedtime', 'A Dragonfly' and 'Good Night' by Eleanor Farjeon from *Silver Sand and Snow* (Michael Joseph) and 'There are Big Waves' by Eleanor Farjeon from *Then There Were Three* (Michael Joseph), all reprinted by permission of David Higham Associates Ltd; 'Gone' by Eric Finney from *Twinkle Twinkle Chocolate Bar* (Oxford University Press, 1991), copyright © Eric Finney, reprinted by permission of Eric Finney; 'At Night' from *Out in the Dark and Daylight* by Aileen Fisher, copyright © 1980 Aileen Fisher; 'Hideout' from *In the Woods, In the Meadow, In the Sky* by Aileen Fisher, copyright © 1965, 1997 Aileen Fisher, both are reprinted by permission of Marian Reiner for the author; 'The Pasture' from *The Poetry of Robert Frost* edited by Edward Connery Latham (Jonathan Cape/Henry Holt and Company, LLC), copyright 1939, © 1967, 1969 by Henry Holt and Co. LLC, reprinted by permission of Random House UK Limited on behalf of the Estate of Robert Frost and Henry Holt and Company, LLC; 'Awkward Child', 'Hen's Song' and 'Witch, Witch' by Rose Fyleman, reprinted by permission of The Society of Authors as the literary representative of the Estate of Rose Fyleman; 'The Dark' by Adrian Henri first published in *The Rhinestone Rhino* (Methuen Books, 1989), copyright © 1989, reprinted by permission of the author c/o Rogers, Coleridge and White Ltd., 20 Powis Mews, London W11 1JN; 'Brother' and 'Tiger' from *The Llama Who Had No Pajama* by Mary Ann Hoberman (Browndeer Press/Harcourt Brace, 1998), copyright © 1959 by Mary Ann and Norman Hoberman, renewed 1987, 1998 by Mary Ann Hoberman, reprinted by permission of Gina Maccoby Literacy Agency and Harcourt, Inc.; Extract from 'My Donkey' from *What is the Truth?* by Ted Hughes (Faber & Faber Ltd), reprinted by permission of Faber & Faber Ltd; 'Breakfast' by P. H. Kilby from *Sit on the Roof and Holler* (Bell & Hyman Ltd, 1984), copyright © 1984, reprinted by permission of the author; 'Honey Bear' by Elizabeth Lang from *Book of a Thousand Poems* (Evans Brothers, 1942), reprinted by permission of HarperCollins Publishers; 'Good Night, Good Night' from *Jelly Belly* (Macmillan of Canada, 1983), copyright © 1983 Dennis Lee, with permission of the author; 'Celebration' by Alonzo Lopez from *Whispering Wind* by Terry Allen, copyright © 1972 by the Institute of American Indian Arts, used by permission of Doubleday, a division of Random House Inc.; 'Kitty' and 'Thank You, Dad, for Everything' from

ACKNOWLEDGEMENTS

The Fed Up Family Album by Doug MacLeod, reprinted by permission of Penguin Books Australia; 'Goodness Gracious from *Nonstop Nonsense* ' by Margaret Mahy (Orion Children's Books) and 'My Sister' from *The First Margaret Mahy Storybook* by Margaret Mahy (Orion Children's Books), reprinted by permission of Orion Children's Books; 'Catapillow' from *Imaginary Menagerie* by Roger McGough (Viking, 1988), copyright © Roger McGough, 1988; 'Mrs Moon' from *Sky in the Pie* by Roger McGough (Kestrel, 1983), copyright © Roger McGough, 1983, both reprinted by permission of the Peters, Fraser and Dunlop Group Limited on behalf of Roger McGough; 'Going to Sleep' by Ian McMillan from *Twinkle Twinkle Chocolate Bar* (Oxford University Press, 1991), copyright © 1991 Ian McMillan, reprinted by permission of the author; 'Toaster Time' from *There is No Rhyme For Silver* by Eve Merriam, copyright © 1962, 1990 Eve Merriam, reprinted by permission of Marian Reiner; 'Rickety Train Ride' by Tony Mitton, first published in *A Noisy Noise Annoys* (The Bodley Head, 1996), reprinted by permission of the author; 'Dragon Smoke', 'Sometimes' and 'Until I Saw the Sea' by Lilian Moore from *I Feel the Same Way* by Lilian Moore, copyright © 1967, 1995 Lilian Moore, used by permission of Marian Reiner for the author; 'Granny Goat' by Brian Moses from *Twinkle Twinkle Chocolate Bar* (Oxford University Press, 1991), © Brian Moses 1999, reprinted by permission of the poet; 'Biking' from *Midnight Forest and Other Poems* by Judith Nicholls (Faber & Faber Ltd), reprinted by permission of Faber & Faber Ltd; 'Picnic' from *Dragonsfire* by Judith Nicholls (Faber & Faber, 1990) and 'Sounds Good' from *Higgledy-Humbug* by Judith Nicholls (Mary Glasgow Publications, 1990), copyright © Judith Nicholls 1990, both reprinted by permission of the author; 'Don't Cry Caterpillar' and 'Sugarcake Bubble' from *No Hickory No Dickory No Dock* (Viking, 1991) and 'Granny Granny Please Comb My Hair' from *Come Into My Tropical Garden* by Grace Nichols (A & C Black, 1988), reproduced with permission of Curtis Brown Ltd, London, on behalf of Grace Nichols, copyright Grace Nichols 1988, 1991; 'Daddy Fell Into The Pond' by Alfred Noyes, reprinted by permission of John Murray (Publishers) Ltd.; 'Marbles in My Pocket' by Lydia Pender from *Morning Magpie* (Angus and Robertson, 1984), copyright © 1957, reprinted by kind permission of the author, Lydia Pender; 'Roger was a Razor Fish' by Al Pittman from *Down By Jim Long's Stage*, published by Breakwater, St John's, Newfoundland, © the author 1976; Extract from *The Bed Book* by Sylvia Plath (Faber & Faber Ltd), reprinted by permission of Faber & Faber Ltd; 'Run a Little' © James Reeves from *Complete Poems for Children* (Heinemann), reprinted by permission of the James Reeves Estate; 'I am an Apple' and 'The Wobbling Race' by Clive Riche from *Poetry Corner* (BBC Books), permission granted by Clive Riche; 'Busy Day' and 'Going Through the Old Photos' by Michael Rosen from *You Tell Me: Poems by Roger McGough and Michael Rosen* (Kestrel, 1979), copyright © Michael Rosen, 1979, both reprinted by permission of Penguin Books Ltd; 'My Dad's Thumb' from *Mind Your Own Business* (Scholastic Books Ltd) by Michael Rosen © Michael Rosen, reprinted by permission of Scholastic Books Ltd; 'The Tickle Rhyme' by Ian Serraillier from *The Monster Horse* (Oxford University Press, 1950), copyright 1950, reprinted by permission of Anne Serraillier; 'Teddy Has a Fright' by Charles Thomson from *Another Very First Poetry Book* (Oxford University Press, 1992), copyright © Charles Thomson 1992, reprinted by permission of the author; 'Listen' by Telcine Turner from *Song of the Surreys* (Macmillan Publishers, 1977), copyright © 1977, reprinted by permission of the author; 'Giant' by Clive Webster from *Twinkle, Twinkle Chocolate Bar* (Oxford University Press, 1991) reprinted by permission of the author; 'Dad and the Cat and the Tree' and 'Nutter' from *Rabbiting On* by Kit Wright (Collins, 1978), reprinted by permission of the author; 'Little Bird' from River Winding by Charlotte Zolotow, copyright © 1970 by Charlotte Zolotow, reprinted by permission of S©ott Treimel New York.

Every effort has been made to trace copyright holders but in a few cases this has proved impossible. The editor and publishers apologize for these cases of copyright transgression and would like to hear from any copyright holder not acknowledged.

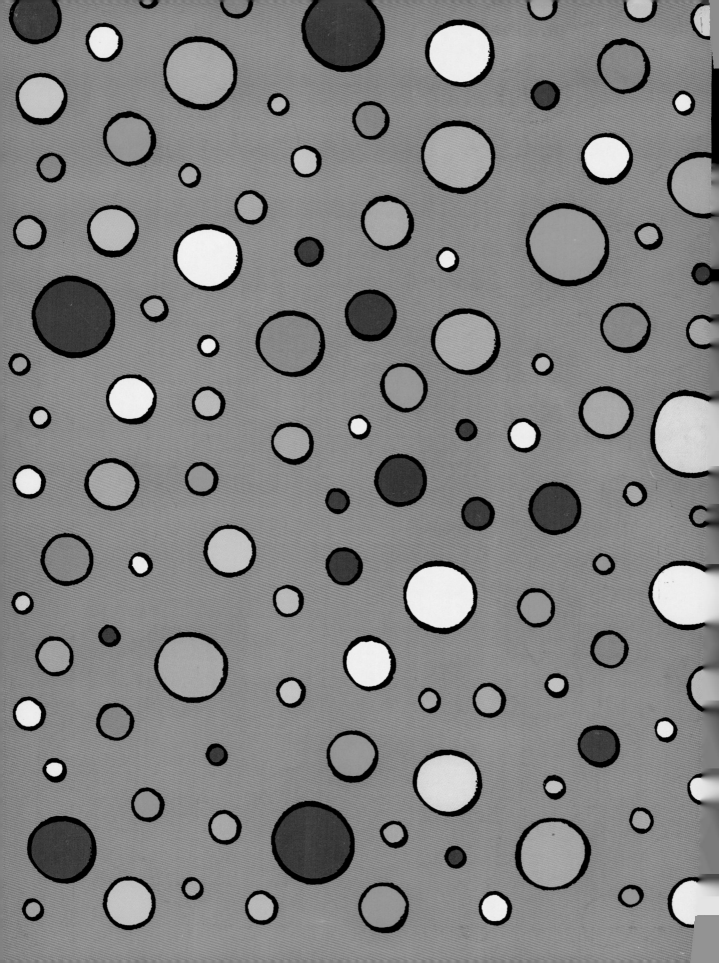